The Glitz Girls

Maureen Haselhurst
Illustrated by Susan Aiello

Rigby
A Harcourt Achieve Imprint

www.Rigby.com
1-800-531-5015

Literacy by Design Leveled Readers: *The Glitz Girls*

ISBN-13: 978-1-4189-3927-4
ISBN-10: 1-4189-3927-7

Printed in China
1A 2 3 4 5 6 7 8 985 13 12 11 10 09 08 07

Contents

Chapter One
The First Day

A school bus nosed its way through a murky Monday morning, nearly empty except for a girl sitting in the first row, huddled into her winter coat and staring out the window.

As the bus jerked to a halt at the street corner, the driver asked, "So, Ellie, it's your first day, huh?" and startled the girl so much that she nearly jumped out of her seat.

"Oh, I'm fine," replied Ellie, "but how do you know my name—and that I'm new here?"

"Well, I know all the kids on my bus, and I've never seen you, which means you have to be new to Summerville Middle School. Plus you've got *Ellie* knitted into your hat. I never met a hat called Ellie, so I just figured that must be your name."

Ellie smiled and yanked the hat off her head, suddenly remembering that it was one that her grandmother had made and knitted her name into.

With a whoosh, the door opened and two girls scrambled aboard, trailed by a tall, thin boy with shaggy brown hair. The girls headed to the back, but the boy sat behind Ellie, leaned forward, and said, "You must be Ellie."

Ellie twisted around in her seat, returned the boy's smile, and asked, "Yes, but who are you and how come everyone seems to know my name?"

"I'm Harry Whitehead, and you're going to be in my class. Mrs. Harland, our teacher, said to be on the lookout for you— especially since you picked such a crazy time to start."

Before Harry could explain, the bus jerked to a stop again, and a noisy stream of kids piled onboard.

Instead of continuing his conversation with Ellie, Harry said loudly, "Hey, you guys, pipe down and meet the new girl!"

The phrase "new girl" caught everyone's attention, and a dozen pairs of eyes suddenly fixed upon Ellie as Harry started the introductions. Soon Ellie's head was spinning as she tried to attach names to faces: Leon Lewis (serious and solemn); Leyla Cheznik (blonde and giggly); Ana Sanchez (small and friendly); and two or three others whose names she had already forgotten.

"I can't believe you're starting today, of all days," said Ana, again leaving Ellie to wonder what was so special about the day. However, she didn't get a chance to ask because Harry was busy introducing her to another batch of students who had just gotten on the bus.

The bus screeched to a halt at an empty corner, but a minute later, the driver shook his head, muttered "Late again," and started to close the door. However, when Harry yelled, "He's coming!" the driver sighed, opened the door again, and waited for a tall boy to climb up the steps.

"Did you sleep in again, Robson?" someone called, but the boy's only response was to swagger down the aisle, chanting a clever rap about a broken alarm clock and a warm bed.

Robson squeezed into the seat across from Harry, glanced at Ellie briefly, said "Hi," and then closed his eyes.

Feeling a bit overwhelmed, Ellie sat quietly, able to hear enough of the talk around her to know that something was going on, and that everyone was looking forward to whatever it was.

As she sat there, Ellie couldn't help but overhear a spirited conversation between Leyla and Ana, who spoke loudly as they discussed "special outfits" they were going to wear and how someone named Jaz had helped them make their choices.

Jaz was mentioned so often and in such admiring terms that Ellie couldn't help wondering about the girl and whether or not she was in Mrs. Harland's class, too.

Ten minutes later, the bus pulled into a paved parking lot, coughed twice, and stopped. The minute the bus door opened, Robson rocketed out of his seat and charged down the stairs like a funky Pied Piper. As

Robson headed toward the school,
he rapped,

"Okay, you guys, time to hit the street.
"Gotta feel the music; gotta feel the beat!"

Ellie walked slowly, her stomach in knots
as she thought about the day ahead of
her. Everyone seemed friendly enough, but
it was still a strange school filled with a
bunch of strange kids, and something
was going on that she knew absolutely
nothing about.

"Good luck today, Ellie!" shouted
the driver just before the bus door
squeezed shut.

And that was the beginning of Ellie
Farthing's first day as a fifth-grader at
Summerville Middle School.

Chapter Two
Meet the Glitz Girls

The parking lot where the bus had
stopped was behind a two-story building
of gray stone with a wide sidewalk that
led to the front of the school. Ellie decided
that Summerville might live up to its name
in the summer, but today the sun seemed
determined to hide, and the town was
enveloped in a puddle of fog.

Ana grabbed one of Ellie's arms and
Leyla grabbed the other, leading her down
the sidewalk behind Robson and Harry, who
were laughing at some joke. The two girls
invited Ellie to help them work on a dance
they were perfecting, which seemed to
consist of two steps to the left, two steps to
the right, hop, hop. Ellie's legs got tangled
with Leyla's on the second hop, and all
three girls started to laugh.

When she stopped laughing, Ana
suggested that they save their dancing for

later and worry about their music instead. That made Ellie curious, and she asked, "What kind of music are you guys into?"

Ana's eyes widened with surprise, then she said, "Of course, you're new, so you couldn't possibly know about our girl band, the Glitz Girls."

"It's the two of us plus Jaz, who plays the keyboard and sings, and who started the band last year," added Leyla. "We're actually kind of famous, at least at school."

"Mostly because of Jaz," said Ana with a laugh. "We wouldn't have a chance of winning the contest without her because she has a fantastic voice and Leyla and I are only good at backup."

"Winning *what* contest?" asked Ellie, hoping that at last she was going to hear what was going on at the middle school.

Leyla and Ana explained that the yearly Summerville Music Festival was just starting and that everything else, even their regular classes, would be on hold for the week while the students went to demonstrations, concerts, and other musical events.

Then Ana added, "But the very best part is the talent contest because you can do any kind of act, as long as it's music of some sort."

"Robson will be dancing and rapping and, of course, the Glitz Girls will perform an act we've been practicing for weeks," said Leyla.

"There's Jaz!" interrupted Ana as the three girls rounded the corner, and then she and Leyla took off at a run, pausing only long enough to tell Ellie to hurry up because she just *had* to meet Jaz.

Ellie followed them, half excited and half nervous at the thought of meeting the wonderful and talented Jaz. The outside of the building was drab, with wide stone steps leading up to a large double door.

However, light and music flooded from every window, and stretched over the door was a colorful banner that read "Summerville Music Festival."

"Ellie, come on!" called Ana, who was standing with Leyla off to one side of the wide stone steps. Ellie headed that

way, unable to spot anyone who might be Jaz. Then Ana stepped aside, revealing a girl with wild, curly red hair sitting in a wheelchair.

After Leyla made the introductions, Jaz smiled and welcomed Ellie to Summerville Middle School. Then a bell rang, and clumps of kids streamed into the building as Jaz swiveled and steered her chair up a ramp beside the steps with Ana and Leyla talking and giggling beside her.

The next few hours were a blur for Ellie. She was assigned a locker, taken on a confusing tour of the building, given a schedule that she was told wouldn't be followed this week, and directed to a desk at the back of the room, near Leyla, Ana, and Jaz.

But the real shock of the day came when her teacher, Mrs. Harland, said, "I know it's terribly last minute, Ellie, but would you be at all interested in entering the talent show?"

Ellie considered for a moment before saying, "Well, I can play piano and sing a little, so I guess I could enter."

The next thing she knew, she was signed up to compete as a solo artist and told that the first round would take place the next day. When Ellie gasped at that news, Mrs. Harland assured her that she didn't need to worry because participating was the important thing, not winning.

As Mrs. Harland walked off, making notes on a clipboard, Jaz said, "Winning *is* important, Ellie, because only the acts that win tomorrow go on to the final round." Then she looked at Ana and Leyla and added, "Which means we should head to the auditorium now for some serious practicing—and to see if we can find a piano for Ellie to use."

Chapter Three

Doo-Wop Decibels

As the girls headed down the hallway, music of every style and degree of loudness seeped out of the classrooms they passed. There were kids everywhere, popping in and out of rooms, and almost all toting instruments, music stands, or sheet music.

As soon as the girls reached the school auditorium, Leyla headed straight for the stage, dashed up a short set of steps, and reached for the rope that controlled the curtains. But before she could pull them open, the curtains twitched apart, a face appeared, and Harry said, "You can't have the stage now because I signed up for this time slot."

This announcement was followed by a lot of teasing and begging on the part of the girls, in an attempt to convince Harry that he just had to reveal his "secret" talent show act to them.

At first Harry protested that part of his act still needed a lot of work, but then he finally gave in, told the girls to wait for a few minutes, and disappeared behind the heavy curtains. His audience listened intently as a wheezing, gasping noise was quickly followed by a lot of twanging, jingling, and thumping.

When a muffled voice finally gave the

go-ahead, Leyla pulled the rope and the curtains parted in a cloud of dust, revealing Harry standing on the stage with his . . .

"What in the world is that pile of junk?" asked Jaz as the other three girls burst out with laughter.

"It's my one-man band, Jaz, not a pile of junk!" Harry protested.

Ellie couldn't believe her eyes as she studied the strange scene before her. Harry's one-man band consisted of an accordion slung across his chest, a bent coat hanger attached to the accordion and supporting a harmonica, and a drum hanging low on his back. He also had a drumstick tied to each heel, a tambourine hanging from one elbow, silver bells hanging from the other, and a second set of bells attached to the top of the knit hat on his head.

"Can you play this thing?" Jaz asked when everyone finally stopped laughing.

"Well, I can play everything pretty well individually, but it's not so easy playing them all at once," Harry admitted. Then he told Leyla to close the curtains again so he could continue practicing in private.

As soon as Harry was once again hidden from all eyes, Ana and Leyla hurried off to get their instruments, leaving Jaz behind to find a quiet spot to rehearse. That wasn't going to be easy to do, Ellie soon realized. She saw several girls singing loudly in one corner, Robson dancing to the rhythm of an electronic drum machine in another corner, and, close by, someone hidden behind a huge set of drums and banging away in a totally different rhythm.

"How in the world do they expect us to practice with all this racket going on?" demanded Jaz, as she wheeled past a girl with a violin and headed straight for Robson, who grinned as she approached.

To Ellie's surprise, Jaz went straight by Robson and pressed a switch to turn off the noisy drum machine.

As the machine fell silent, Robson looked stunned and a bit angry, but quickly recovered and rapped:

"Jaz, my friend, you're being a child
"For picking on me when the others
are wild."

However, Jaz clearly didn't intend to only pick on Robson, because she swiveled her chair, wheeled up to the drum set, and shouted, "QUIET!"

When the drummer slowly got to his feet, Jaz gasped and said, "Leon, I thought all you did was read and study, but here you are playing the drums!"

While Leon complained loudly about having his rhythm broken, Robson studied his classmate intently and finally said, "Leon, that funky number you were playing makes me think that if the two of us joined forces we could win this contest."

A startled Leon responded, "You're nuts if you think I'm letting you steal my 'Doo-Wop Decibels' for your act."

Jaz whispered, "Robson must mean it because the only time he doesn't talk in rhyme is when the teachers won't let him—or when he's really serious about something."

Meanwhile, Robson was smiling and saying, "I'm talking about performing together, Leon, not about stealing your song from you. After all, it's plain to see that you can drum like a major rock star, and you know that I can rap and dance like no one else can. So do you think you might see a band with a name like Pizzazz in your future?"

At first, Leon's expression was hard to read, but at last he smiled and said, "You're on, Robson, my friend!"

Chapter Four
Practice Makes Perfect

"Here we are!" announced Leyla as she hurried up to Jaz and Ellie, carrying a trombone case in one hand and pushing a keyboard on wheels with the other.

"We couldn't find a piano, Ellie," said Ana, who was lugging a bass guitar that was almost her size, "but Mrs. Harland said to tell you that there would be a piano on the stage tomorrow for sure, and that you could use this keyboard when we're done with it today."

Since Ellie couldn't practice yet, she decided to sit down and watch the others rehearse. Harry, who had decided to open the curtains to entertain a bunch of kids with his wacky band, was having trouble keeping the harmonica in the right position. In the corner, Leon was playing "Doo-Wop Decibels" softly while Robson composed a rap to accompany the music.

However, once Jaz, Leyla, and Ana started to rehearse, most of the other performers stopped their own practices to watch the Glitz Girls in action. As the trio played, Ana was almost hidden by her huge guitar, Jaz sat confidently behind the keyboard, and Leyla handled her trombone like a born musician. The odd combination of instruments sounded wonderful together, especially when Jaz's sweet, husky voice began to fill the auditorium, softly supported by Leyla and Ana's backup singing, which was much better than they had led Ellie to believe.

Quietly Harry slid into the seat next to

Ellie and said, "I don't know why anyone else bothers to enter the Girl Band category, because no one stands a chance against these three."

Several minutes later, a bell rang in three short bursts, and the Glitz Girls stopped playing as everyone packed up instruments, folded music stands, and organized their music. Robson walked past Ellie, grinned at her, and delivered his rap.

"Why, Ellie girl, you should be playin',
"But the day's over and there's no stayin'."

Ana groaned in dismay at Robson's rap and came up to Ellie with a worried look on her face. "We really didn't mean to hog the keyboard," she said, "but we didn't realize how late it was, Ellie. Why don't you come on over to Jaz's house tonight to practice on her keyboard while we're working on our outfits for the show?"

Jaz didn't appear overly enthusiastic about Ana's idea, but she nodded slowly and said, "Come on over if you want to, Ellie."

However, Ellie just shook her head and said, "My mom teaches music, so we have a piano at home and I can practice tonight."

"Well, I can't wait to hear you play, Ellie," said Ana with a smile.

Then Leyla gestured toward the door and said, "We have to grab our stuff and get to the buses, guys, or we'll miss our rides home."

All four girls headed for their lockers, grabbed their coats and belongings, and hurried outside to the crowded sidewalk. At the end of the ramp, Jaz went to her bus while Ellie followed Leyla and Ana around the corner to the parking lot and a long line of yellow buses sending steamy smoke signals into the winter air.

Chapter Five

The First Round

The next morning, the bus repeated its now-familiar route, with Harry getting on soon after Ellie, Ana and Leyla boarding at the next stop with Leon, and Robson, as usual, almost missing the bus.

"Can we squeeze in with you?" asked Ana, dropping her purple backpack on the seat beside Ellie and shaking snow from her hat.

Ellie smiled, nodded, and moved a bit closer to the window, thinking that only 24 hours ago, she had been a stranger, and now she felt like she had at least two friends. She wasn't so sure that she'd call Jaz a friend, however.

Soon Ellie was listening to the two girls talk about their talent show outfits and answering their questions about the musical pieces she had practiced with her mother. And before she knew it, the ride was over.

As usual, Jaz was waiting by the ramp when the girls rounded the corner. Today, to Ellie's surprise, Jaz smiled and asked, "Are you ready for the show, Ellie?"

Ellie nodded, then all four girls went inside, shed their coats, and headed to the auditorium to meet Mrs. Harland. The huge room was filled with the noise of students tuning instruments in a concert of squeaks and toots and tapping out electronic SOS messages as they tested microphones. In the middle of this uproar, Mrs. Harland was standing on the stage, waving her arms, and saying something that no one could possibly hear.

"I see the sign for Girl Bands," Leyla announced, "and the Solo Artists section is right next to that, Ellie."

The four girls headed off to the other side of the auditorium, and the noise gradually dulled as everyone found their seats.

"I realize how excited you all must be this morning," Mrs. Harland was saying loudly, "but we have some important housekeeping to do before we can get under way."

Mrs. Harland paused and stared sternly at the chattering students for several long moments, until finally neighbor nudged neighbor and the entire room was hushed and attentive.

In a more normal voice, Mrs. Harland explained that today they would be performing for themselves and the judges, rather than for a formal audience, with the grade-level winners in each category going on to the final competition on Friday.

"And now," she said, "it's time at last to meet our three talented judges: Wanda Slovaka, director of the State Ballet Company; Professor Harley Houseman, head of the Summerville Music Academy; and Justin Credible, music reporter for *The Summerville Times*."

Everyone clapped politely as a tiny woman dressed in black velvet, a large man with a shaggy gray beard, and a young man with spiky purple hair joined Mrs. Harland up on the stage.

The young man, whom Ellie decided had

to be Justin Credible, waved madly and pointed to the front of his T-shirt, which read, "Music Rocks Me!"

At last the applause died down, and the three judges left the stage to take their seats in the first row, right in front of the stage. It was time for the first round of the Summerville Music Festival talent show to begin!

Chapter Six
Unexpected Competition

For Ellie, the next hour and a half was a combination of magic moments—listening to the performances—and nervous moments—waiting as the clock crawled toward the last act of the day, which would be hers. Just one row in front of her, the Glitz Girls were also waiting, but as far as Ellie could tell, none of them seemed at all nervous about their upcoming performance.

Leon, on the other hand, looked like Ellie felt as he chewed on a fingernail and beat a drumstick against his leg in a rhythm that seemed intended to accompany Robson's eyes-closed mouthing of the rap lyrics to "Doo-wop Decibels."

From the other side of the room, Harry caught Ellie's eye, grinned widely, and gave her a thumbs-up gesture which she returned before sitting back to enjoy yet another performance.

When it was finally time for the fifth-grade performances to begin, Mrs. Harland announced that Pizzazz would be first, and Leon and Robson took to the stage to shouts of "Go for it, guys!"

Soon the two boys had the entire student body snapping fingers, clapping, and gasping as Robson spun like a top on the wooden stage. By the end of their song, even the judges were nodding their heads to the beat, and Leon and Robson finished their act to the sound of thunderous applause.

The Glitz Girls were next, and Leyla and Ana waved to Ellie as they followed Jaz up the ramp. For a full minute, all three girls looked out at the audience in silence. Then Ana strummed a low chord on her guitar, followed by a few chords from Jaz's keyboard, and, at last, a haunting note from Leyla's trombone.

A few bars into the music, Jaz leaned toward the microphone and started to sing, sounding even better to Ellie than she had the day before. Everyone else seemed to agree because there was hardly a whisper from the audience, with even the judges sitting forward and listening intently.

As the music trailed off and the students burst into applause, Professor Houseman leaned toward Wanda Slovaka to say something, and Justin Credible jumped out of his seat in excitement.

When the room finally became quiet again, Mrs. Harland announced the fifth-grade Wild Card performance, and Harry and his wacky band clanked onstage. To Ellie's delight, Harry had finally mastered all the elements of his band and managed to make the accordion, harmonica, drums, tambourine, and bells behave as he intended. When he finished and took a noisy bow, the room rocked with laughter and applause.

After several more performances, Ellie was climbing the steps to the stage, wondering what she had been thinking to agree to compete in a contest with students who had been practicing their music for weeks. She had never even touched the piano that now waited for her, and she was sure she would make a complete fool of herself.

At last Ellie reached the piano and sat on the bench with her head down, feeling hundreds of eyes upon her and listening as a low murmur of sound filled the auditorium. She ran her fingers over the keys soundlessly, replaying her mother's voice as it said, "Just think about the music, Ellie, not about the audience."

Ellie took a deep breath and started to play, her notes timid at first. Then she gained confidence as the music flowed from her fingers to the ears of the now-quiet audience.

Then Ellie began to sing in a light, pure voice quite different from Jaz's low, husky sound, but equally lovely to hear. Her listeners leaned forward in their seats, intent on every word.

Ellie's last notes hung in the air for a moment. Then she smiled shyly, bowed, and headed down the steps, accompanied by loud applause and more than a few cheers.

In the audience, Leyla turned to Jaz and asked, "Do you think that Ellie wrote that song herself?"

Jaz frowned, shook her head, and replied sharply, "She said her mother teaches music, so I'll bet her mother wrote the song."

"Whoever the songwriter is, the song is great," said Ana; then she turned to Ellie, who was just walking by, and called, "That was super, Ellie!" Leyla and several other classmates echoed Ana's compliment, but Jaz was noticeably silent.

A low, excited buzz filled the auditorium while the judges consulted with one another for what seemed more like days than minutes. Finally Professor Houseman got to his feet and lumbered onto the stage. He cleared his throat noisily, and went on to name the winners of each category for seventh grade and then sixth grade, pausing annoyingly before each announcement, as judges often do.

After much cheering, he went on to announce the fifth-grade winners, and when Pizzazz won in the Boy Band category, Robson jumped up from his seat and pumped an arm in the air while Leon waved his drumsticks happily.

As soon as the excitement died down, Professor Houseman continued, saying, "The standard of the Girl Bands was very high, but the judges have agreed that the band advancing to the next level is . . . the Glitz Girls!"

The three girls flung their arms around each other. The crowd cheered and whistled, stopping only when Professor Houseman shouted, "And the winner in the Wild Card category is . . ."

"Harry!" bellowed the audience before the professor could state the obvious, and Harry waved and shook his head, setting the bells on his hat into motion.

By this time, many students were out of their seats, talking, cheering, and laughing loudly. Meanwhile, on the stage, Professor Houseman looked so lost that Mrs. Harland bustled up to join him, waved her arms, and shouted, "Settle down, everyone!"

As order slowly returned to the room, Professor Houseman consulted the sheet of paper he held and said, "There were many outstanding performances in the Solo Artist category. However, the winner is . . . "

Ellie leaned forward, wondering who would be moving on to the next part of the competition.

"Ellie Farthing," he announced.

"Way to go, Ellie!" shouted Robson from the other side of the room, while Ana and Leyla dashed from their seats to give her a joint hug.

Ana stepped back, laughed, and said, "Well, the good news is that you can go to finals with us."

"And the bad news is that you're going to be pretty tough competition for the overall prize," added Leyla with a smile.

Ellie congratulated Ana and Leyla on their win, then watched them head back to their seats where Jaz sat quietly in her wheelchair, her head bent.

"Don't mind Jaz," a quiet voice said, and Ellie turned to see Harry standing next to her. "She's not used to competition," he continued.

Though Jaz couldn't possibly have heard Harry, this was when she turned and raised her head. She gave Ellie a long, unsmiling look that wasn't exactly unfriendly but was close to it.

Chapter Seven
The Green Monster

Wednesday morning's bus ride was an exciting one for Ellie. Her performance had made her a familiar face, and as kids got on, they all greeted her, most saying something nice about her act, including Leon, who said, "You sure do play a mean piano, Ellie."

"I'm glad you're not in the Girl Band category or I'd have to forget about being friends with you!" said Ana a little later, her friendly smile telling Ellie that she was only kidding.

However, once they arrived at school, it didn't take Ellie long to realize that Jaz's attitude had changed for the worse. Jaz hadn't acted overly friendly before, but she hadn't been exactly unfriendly either; however, today, when Ellie said, "You were great yesterday," Jaz just acted like she hadn't heard and wheeled off to the other side of the room.

"What's with her?" said Ellie under her breath, and, to her horror, Robson overheard. As usual, he responded in rap.

A certain someone is used to being the queen,

"But now she met a monster, and that monster is green."

When Ellie looked puzzled, Robson said, "Hey, I like Jaz, but you gotta understand that she's been Miss Popularity in Summerville forever, and that's partly because of her music."

"So you're saying I'm a monster for entering the contest?" asked Ellie.

Robson laughed and said, "No, I meant a green-eyed monster."

Still puzzled, Ellie shook her head and said, "You're saying she's jealous, which is what Harry kind of said yesterday, but I just don't understand. Why would Jaz be jealous of me when she's so fantastic?"

"Hey, I'm just observing the facts, not explaining them," replied Robson as he walked off.

Wednesday zipped by, and soon school was over and Ellie was restless. At last she said, "Mom, I'm going nuts waiting for tomorrow to come, so can I deliver the music festival flyers we're supposed to pass out in the neighborhood?"

After several warnings from her mother about getting lost and being back home in time for dinner, Ellie left the house and headed into a part of the neighborhood she hadn't really explored yet. Tall trees arched over the street, their bare branches reaching out to welcome Ellie to her new neighborhood as she slipped flyers onto front-door handles.

At one house, as Ellie was slipping a flyer onto the black metal handle, the door suddenly opened and a woman asked, "Can I help you?"

"Oh, I didn't mean to bother you," said Ellie, introducing herself and going on to explain about the flyers and being in the show.

The woman laughed, accepted a flyer, and exclaimed, "Oh, I know all about this because Jaz is in the show, too."

"Jaz Murphy?" asked Ellie, unable to believe what she was hearing. Out of dozens of houses in the neighborhood, why did this have to be the one where someone actually came to the door?

"Well, of course you already know each other, since you're both in the talent show," said Mrs. Murphy, waving the flyer as proof of Ellie's participation. And before Ellie could make a hasty retreat, Jaz's mother had steered her inside and closed the door. She pointed to a wide hallway on the left and said, "Just knock loudly on the first door so the girls can hear you over the music."

All Ellie wanted to do was run, but she couldn't, so she headed down the hall on leaden legs.

Soon Ellie heard music coming from behind a closed door. When she looked back over her shoulder, Mrs. Murphy gave her a friendly wave, then turned and walked away.

Ellie was relieved, thinking that perhaps she could get out of the house without seeing Jaz after all, but as she turned, the music suddenly stopped.

When the sound of her own name filtered through the closed door, Ellie moved closer. She heard Leyla say, "I don't get why you don't like her, Jaz."

"I don't know her, so I can't really like her or dislike her," said Jaz. "All I know is that a week ago, we were sure to win the talent show, and now, along comes Ellie, ready to steal our prize out from under us."

Ana spoke next, saying, "Oh, Jaz, we can still win our category, and we might win overall, too, you know."

"Well, the reason I don't trust her is because she said she could play 'a little,' then she got up there and sounded like a concert performer," said Jaz. "So I wonder what she'll do for the final competition."

More determined than before to get out before she was discovered, Ellie backed away from the door, then glanced toward the living room to be sure Mrs. Murphy hadn't returned. The coast looked clear, so she started to slink down the hallway, but in her nervousness, dropped the clipboard that held the flyers.

If the Glitz Girls had still been playing—or even talking—they never would have noticed when the clipboard thumped against the wooden floor. However, they weren't playing or talking at the moment, and they did notice. Ellie froze as the door flew open and Jaz cried, "What are you doing here?"

"I–I–I–" stammered Ellie, at a loss to explain exactly what she was doing. At last she found her voice and said, "I was delivering flyers and your mother said—"

"You were spying on us!" exclaimed Jaz, interrupting Ellie's rambling explanation. "You're trying to figure out how to beat us in the talent show!"

"But I didn't even know you lived here until your mother told me!" protested Ellie, looking toward Ana and Leyla for support, but seeing no sign of it.

Jaz's response was to shut the door in Ellie's face, leaving her fighting back tears as she hurried to the front door and let herself out. Mrs. Murphy's cheerful, "Come again, Ellie," followed her out the door.

Chapter Eight
The Old Piano

On Thursday Ellie couldn't face seeing Ana and Leyla on the bus, so she convinced her father to drop her off at school a little early, saying she wanted time to practice.

Once the day started, it didn't take long for Ellie to hear the rumor: Ellie Farthing had been spying on the Glitz Girls!

Ellie spent most of the morning sitting quietly in the classroom, avoiding the Glitz Girls. She was grateful that most kids were too excited about the upcoming talent show to spend much time worrying about a spy in their midst.

Late in the morning, Mrs. Harland noticed how quiet Ellie was, and said, "Ellie, you seem so down and out amid all the excitement."

"Mrs. Harland, can I pull out of the finals, please?" asked Ellie.

"You were wonderful yesterday, Ellie, and the program is already printed, so you can't pull out now," said Mrs. Harland. "Everyone gets a little nervous before a competition, but you can't let that stop you, Ellie."

When Ellie didn't reply, Mrs. Harland said, "You just need to keep busy until it's time for the show, so you can help me out, if you're willing."

Ellie shrugged her agreement, and then listened as her teacher explained about needing more microphones and not having time to get to the equipment room to look for them.

So a few minutes later, Ellie was making her way down a long hall and past the cafeteria, looking for room 151. When she reached it, she inserted the key, unlocked the door, and pushed against it, almost tumbling inside.

"What a mess!" marveled Ellie as she looked around at the boxes, bins, and crates piled on the floor and on crooked wooden shelves that lined the walls. Stacks of yellowed sheet music offered evidence that no one had bothered to clean out the room in years.

As Ellie entered the room, she spotted an old piano covered by a dingy sheet, but still recognizable.

Unable to resist, Ellie removed the sheet and lifted the lid to expose worn and chipped ivory keys. She found a stool, brushed a thick layer of dust from its surface, and pulled it up to the piano before sitting down and pressing a few keys. The sound was better than she had expected. Soon she was coaxing a favorite tune from the old instrument, her errand forgotten.

Meanwhile, Mrs. Harland, who was waiting for the extra microphones, found Jaz in the hallway and said, "I sent Ellie to the equipment room ages ago. Could you go and check to see if she found the microphones I wanted?"

Jaz couldn't tell Mrs. Harland that Ellie was the last person she wanted to see, so she set out to find her. As she got close to the equipment room, Jaz realized that lovely music was tumbling out the half-open door.

Jaz entered the room silently and saw

Ellie playing the beat-up piano. How could anyone make such an ugly, old instrument sound so good? she thought. And how could she compete with someone who could?

For a moment, it occurred to Jaz that it would be very easy to quietly close the door and use the key Ellie had left in the lock to shut her in, which would put an end to any competition from the new girl.

But Jaz never seriously considered doing such an awful thing. She was a musician, and, drawn in by the beauty of Ellie's music, she just sat there, listening to a private concert.

Chapter Nine
Trapped!

With a sudden BANG, the heavy wooden door slammed shut, followed by a giggle and the sound of footsteps in the hall. Startled, Ellie screamed, jumped up from the piano bench, and discovered Jaz by the door, looking equally startled.

"What are you doing here, and why did you slam the door?" demanded Ellie.

In a shaky voice, Jaz responded, "Those footsteps in the hall should tell you that this is someone's idea of a really bad joke, Ellie."

Ellie shrugged and said, "OK, so you didn't slam the door, but I still want to know what you're doing here, other than spying on me, I mean."

Then the reason for Jaz's presence dawned on her, and she said, "Oh, I completely forgot about the microphones!"

Ellie hurried over to the corner, looked at the labeled boxes, and grabbed the microphones. Ignoring Jaz, she headed to the door, but when she turned the knob, nothing happened.

"You left the key in the lock and someone has locked us in!" cried Jaz, who was now so pale that her freckles stood out like polka dots.

"OK," said Ellie, clearly addressing herself as well as Jaz, "there's no need to panic because someone is sure to come looking for us."

Suddenly a bell sounded, signaling the end of the school day. Jaz wheeled over to the only window that was clear of junk and looked outside toward the front steps where a stream of students was leaving the building.

"Everyone's going home!" Ellie cried, then dashed over to Jaz and tried to open the window, which was stuck fast by years and layers of paint.

Then Ellie ran for the door and started hammering on the thick wood with her fist while Jaz shouted through the closed window, "Get us out of here!"

The girls kept hammering and shouting until Jaz announced in a gloomy voice, "There goes the last bus—and our last chance to get out of here."

"My mom won't miss me because she's coming to the show straight from work," said Ellie, sounding hopeless.

"And I told my mom I might go home with Ana," moaned Jaz.

Ellie sighed, sank down by the door, and said, "At least people will be coming back for tonight's show, so we'll get rescued then."

Darkness comes early in winter, and as light slowly seeped out of the room, Ellie got up to turn on the light. But when she flipped the switch on, nothing happened.

"We're trapped in the dark!" said Jaz, a touch of panic in her voice.

Ellie was quiet for a moment before asking softly, "Are you afraid of the dark like I am?"

At first Jaz denied feeling scared, but then she finally said, "OK, so I guess we have something in common after all."

"Let's not talk about the dark, then," said Ellie as she rose and made her way through the dim light to the piano, where she ran her fingers over the keys. Turning to Jaz, she asked, "What was that song you guys did on Tuesday?"

"You mean this one?" said Jaz, tapping out a tune on the arm of her wheelchair.

Ellie nodded, moved the bench over to make room for Jaz's wheelchair, and said, "Maybe music will make the time go faster."

Two hours later, the girls were still sitting at the old piano, but now they were talking instead of playing. When Ellie tried to explain that she hadn't been spying, Jaz admitted that she never really believed that Ellie was a spy, and that she didn't really know why she had ever said such a thing.

"We both love music, and we live near each other, and . . . " said Ellie a few minutes later, her voice trailing off into the darkness.

"And we should be friends—you and me and Leyla and Ana," said Jaz. Then she laughed and declared, "Friends forever!" She accompanied her words with a low, loud *dum-dum-dum-DUM* on the piano.

The notes echoed through the darkness just as Harry, a bit uneasy about entering the dark building, arrived to make some last-minute adjustments to his one-man band.

While Harry was wondering if he should make a hasty retreat and wait outside until someone else showed up, a series of even louder *dum-dum-dum-DUMs* made him more curious than afraid.

"After all," he said out loud, "it's not like a burglar is going to be thumping on a piano." Reassured by the sound of his own voice, Harry started down the hall in the direction of the loud sound.

That's how he found Ellie and Jaz, who were laughing when the door opened.

Blinking in the sudden light, Ellie shouted, "Harry, are we glad to see you!"

"What are you two doing here?" Harry asked, surprise evident in his voice.

Ellie and Jaz quickly explained about the microphones and the footsteps in the hall and watching everyone leave them behind, laughing and tripping over one another's words as they told Harry about their adventures in the dark.

"Well, it's almost time for the show, so you guys had better get moving," said Harry when they finished.

"I still have to change into my show outfit," groaned Jaz.

"Yes, me, too. But we missed dinner. We've got to eat something before we perform," said Ellie.

"You're in luck, girls! I didn't finish my lunch today so if you don't mind soggy peanut butter, dinner's on me," said Harry as he led the way down the hall.

Chapter Ten

The Glitz Girls Onstage

The auditorium was buzzing with noise as people settled into their seats. The room set aside for waiting contestants was buzzing, too, and a lot of the buzz came from Leyla and Ana, who were wondering why Ellie was missing and where Jaz had gotten to.

Ana said, "Jaz said she might come to my house, but she didn't show up after school, so I figured she went home."

Leyla added, "I don't know what Ellie had planned, but I tried to call Jaz after school and her mother said she was at your house."

"We can't perform without Jaz!" wailed Ana.

Just then, Harry came in and announced, "Look who I found," as Ellie and Jaz followed him into the room, each chewing on half of Harry's leftover peanut butter sandwich.

"I need a drink, so I'll let Ellie explain everything to you," said Jaz, clearing her throat. Soon Leyla and Ana had the whole story—including the news of the friendship that had blossomed in the dark.

When Ana commented that it was lucky they had gotten out before the show, Ellie smiled sadly and said, "It doesn't really matter because I'm pulling out of the contest." As the others stared at her, Ellie held out her hands, revealing knuckles that were swollen and dark with bruises.

"I guess hammering on a door isn't such a smart thing for a piano player to do," she said.

"Oh, Ellie, I'm sorry," said Jaz in a hoarse voice.

Ana and Leyla looked at her with concern, so Jaz cleared her throat again and said, "I just need to warm up a bit," and then sang a few croaking notes.

Realizing that all the shouting at the window had cost Jaz her voice, Leyla said glumly, "So it looks like the Glitz Girls have to pull out, too!"

"I'm sorry, guys, but I can barely talk now, let alone sing," admitted Jaz in a rough whisper.

The four girls sat in silence, staring blankly into space as everyone around them chattered, tuned up, and practiced their numbers—everyone except Robson, who was staring at them thoughtfully.

At last he said, "OK, Jaz can't sing, that's for sure, but she can still play the keyboard; and Ellie can't play the piano with those hands, but she can still sing, so—"

Jaz started to smile for the first time in an hour, and Ellie jumped up from the floor and shouted, "Robson, you're a genius!"

"Robson, I know you're suggesting that Ellie should sing along with us, which is a great idea except that she doesn't know our song," said Ana.

"Oh, yes, she does," croaked Jaz.

"After all," said Ellie, "what do you think two musicians were doing while stuck for hours in the dark in a room with a piano?"

Leyla jumped up, grabbed Ana, and shouted, "OK, we've got a show to put on!"

So there was a slight change to the program for the Summerville Music Festival. When it was time for the Glitz Girls to perform, Mrs. Harland announced that due to unforeseen circumstances, Ellie Farthing would be performing with the group instead of as a solo artist.

The contest was a great success, with the crowd cheering for every performance, and the judges shaking their heads over the difficult choices they had to make.

Finally Professor Houseman shuffled up the steps and, after much hemming and hawing and plenty of praise for everyone, he said, "The judges are happy to award the prize for Best Overall Act to—"

After a long pause, he continued, "to a most original performer—Harry Whitehead and his one-man band!"

The audience cheered wildly when Harry charged up onto the stage, smiling hugely and accepting his trophy from the professor.

Wanda Slovaka took the microphone next and announced that the prize for Best Overall Dance Talent went to a brand-new band called Pizzazz, for its dazzling drumming and dancing.

Leon and Robson gave each other high-fives all the way up to the stage and back.

Ellie and the Glitz Girls clapped as hard as anyone for their friends, but they couldn't help thinking about what might have been.

"I'm not nearly as good a singer as Jaz, so if she'd been able to sing, you guys probably would have won," said Ellie.

In a raspy voice, Jaz responded, "You were wonderful, Ellie, and in fact, I was even thinking that you—"

Mrs. Harland interrupted Jaz's sentence as she called for attention, saying, "As you know, your votes determine the final prize of the evening—the audience favorite." She turned to Justin Credible, who grinned, stepped up to the microphone, and bellowed, "And the audience's choice is those musical marvels, those wonderful warblers, that quality quartet—the Glitz Girls!"

Ana and Leyla started screaming and jumping up and down, but Jaz just smiled at a stunned Ellie and said, "What I was trying to say before is that it looks like there are four Glitz Girls now, if you want to join us, I mean."

A smile slowly spread across Ellie's face, and she said, "I can't think of a better way to spend time with my friends."

Together, she and Jaz followed Ana and Leyla up to the stage to collect their trophy.